The Embarrassing Parents

The Movie Icon

*She has taken to disaster movies as the bejewelled socialite
who has to fly the plane*

The Embarrassing Parents

SOCIAL STEREOTYPES FROM THE

Telegraph magazine

Victoria Mather
and
Sue Macartney-Snape

JOHN MURRAY

To

John Raymond
with love, respect and immense gratitude
V.M.

and

To

My siblings Timothy, Deborah and Philippa
and in memory of Ewan
S.M-S.

———————

Text copyright © 2000, 2001 and 2002 Daily Telegraph plc
and Victoria Mather

Illustrations copyright © 2000, 2001 and 2002 Daily Telegraph plc
and Sue Macartney-Snape

First published in 2002
by John Murray (Publishers)
A division of Hodder Headline

5 7 9 10 8 6

A CIP catalogue record for this title is available from the British Library

ISBN 0–7195–6231 7

Typeset in 11.5/15pt Monotype Bembo
by Servis Filmsetting Ltd, Manchester

Printed and bound in Spain by
Bookprint S.L., Barcelona

John Murray (Publishers)
338 Euston Road
London
NW1 3BH

Foreword

I NEVER TURN to Victoria Mather's and Sue Macartney-Snape's *Social Stereotypes* in the Saturday *Telegraph* without a creeping anxiety that I might come face to face with myself. It has happened at least five times already: The English Family on Holiday, The Smug Couple from Notting Hill, The Couple Crippled by School Fees, Man Packing the Car Boot and The Couple Who Have Moved to The Country. It is impossible to read them without the flustered suspicion that it is my own life and my own family Victoria and Sue have so vividly in their sights. And here, of course, lies the genius of *Social Stereotypes*. Every Saturday, all over the country, thousands of different people are utterly convinced that they must be the models for The Pony Club Official or The Obsessive Tanner. Victoria and Sue have a mind-reader's gift for rootling around inside our heads, and serving up every last nuance and pretension as spot-on social comedy.

It is a mystery how they get it exactly right, week after week. It isn't that either of them hangs out with most of the groups lampooned with such deadly accuracy in this latest collection. Neither of them belongs to a gentleman's club or spends their weekends going caravanning, or has children at prep school or teenagers who holiday at Rock in Cornwall. I know for a fact that Victoria never flies anywhere in economy class, and shudders at the thought, and yet she instinctively captures the myriad indignities of travelling on the wrong side of the curtain. And how come Sue Macartney-Snape, who pads around bohemian Westbourne Grove in a zebra-skin coat, has such an unerring eye for the school fathers' race or elderly swimmers?

The answer, of course, is that they are brilliantly observant and intuitive, alert to every foible of character, which is the key to all great satire. They are only the latest in a long tradition of British humour which extends as far back as Hogarth, and takes in Wodehouse, Waugh and every film and TV sitcom starring Penelope Keith, Sid James and John le Mesurier. Any foreigner relocating to England for the first time could do no better than study all five volumes of *Social Stereotypes* as the swiftest method of understanding their new neighbours and assimilating our national psyche.

If Sue Macartney-Snape is the new H. M. Bateman or Ronald Searle, it is becoming increasingly obvious that Victoria Mather is Britain's answer to Dorothy Parker. With her cut-throat wit and fondness for double vodka martinis, it is easy to imagine her keeping them spellbound at the Algonquin Round Table, with her pampered Pekingese snuffling about between everyone's legs. There has always been something of the mordant glamour of pre-war Manhattan in Victoria's writing. Had she been a regular at the Algonquin, she would, of course, have swiftly forged a fortuitous friendship with the General Manager of the hotel, and the round table would have been upgraded to some luxurious suite on the Club Floor — for that is another gift of this polymathic reporter, satirist and travel arbiter. One of my favourite Dorothy Parkerisms is, 'As far as I'm concerned, the most beautiful word in the English language is Cellar Door.' Victoria once declared that her own favourite words are 'Private and Jet, but only in sequence'.

In the end, though, it is the particular Englishness of Victoria's ear and Sue's eye which captivate. It isn't widely appreciated that Sue's caricatures are completed first, and then biked round to Victoria's cottage in Battersea where she devises the perfect words to go with them, tailoring her dialogue to the exact specification. Had 'The Mother at Rock', for instance, looked three years older or younger in the caricature, she would have amended the words accordingly, and been every bit as convincing. I like to think of Victoria driving between her numerous homes in Hampshire, Battersea and Cowes, revising the perfectly calibrated dialogue inside her head. Now I come to think of it, she is actually the modern-day Nancy Mitford every bit as much as the modern-day Dorothy Parker.

The collaboration between Mather and Macartney-Snape is a precious British institution, as perfect in its way as Fry and Laurie, Morecambe and Wise, Fortnum & Mason, Gilbert and Sullivan, Holland & Holland or Truslove & Hanson. I do hope they never get round to mobbing-up the stereotypical Glossy Magazine Managing Director in one of their cameos – but I fear it is only a matter of time.

Nicholas Coleridge
Autumn 2002

Acknowledgements

Twenty-five years is a long time in friendship. Nicholas Coleridge is the best of friends, the most loyal colleague and a wise mentor. Only one person has made me laugh more in pursuit of journalistic mischief and that's Emma Soames. Emma espoused Social Stereotypes from the beginning of her reign as editor of the *Telegraph Magazine*; eight years later Sue and I are still part of the furniture. Emma, as befits a witty woman of the world, has moved on to more grown-up things, but we're still there, like Sondheim's *Follies*. Yet the column would be nowhere without the help of Sarah and Johnny Standing, India Leon, Anna McNair Scott, Melissa Alexander, Timothy Lipscomb, Lucy Fox, John Grandy, Caroline Wrey and especially Camilla Osborne, a life-enhancer. Phoebe Bentinck and David Zambra have been the booksellers *extraordinaires* at Henry Stokes in Belgravia. Due to the wonder of modern communications, Stereotypes have pinged to the *Telegraph* from all over the world, but particular thanks to Mark and Moira Andreae and Christopher and Philippa Chetwode, who enabled the column to continue uninterrupted, apart from incisive contributions, at their respective houses in Jamaica and Toulouse. Fielding the drawings and the words from Sydney, Tasmania, Los Angeles, the Maldives and Africa – The Caravanners went on light aircraft with some beer crates to the Okavango's sole fax machine – have been Louise Carpenter and Will Ellsworth-Jones, our patient editors, and Denis Piggott, the stoical production manager. Juliet Caulfield and Sandi Elsden are the voices on the telephone reassuring us that 'The Stereo has landed.' We are proud to be published by John Murray – that this firm extended the same courtesy to Jane Austen, Byron and Osbert Lancaster is to be a small part of publishing history – and very grateful to Caroline Knox for nurturing us in such illustrious company.

Victoria Mather

Gerard views his daughter entirely through his Sony camcorder and Lucy's thrilled she found the Virgin's flipflops in Jigsaw

Parents at the Nativity Play

THE POLITICAL MACHINATIONS that have culminated in Pandora Simpkins standing, stolidly, in front of her parents as the Virgin Mary would awe Colin Powell. It began in October when Pandora returned home with the news that she was to be the star in the school nativity play. Her mother said no one would be a more inspiring madonna than darling Panda. Pandora had had to explain, through strangulated mouthfuls of Marmite sandwich, that she meant the Star of Bethlehem. 'I twinkle.' Lucy Simpkins had been on to the headmistress immediately. 'Mrs Hornsby? This is Pandora's mummy. I've just heard her news about the nativity play, and I am shocked. Last year she gave a very creative interpretation of the innkeeper's wife, improvising her line – improvising, Mrs Hornsby, and she was only five. When the innkeeper turned Mary and Joseph away, Pandora said, "It's a smelly old stable but I can do you room service – have a nice day." I think, Mrs Hornsby, you will agree that she is capable of rather more than twinkling.' Mrs Hornsby had said that the Star of Bethlehem was a crucial, albeit non-speaking, role. Lucy retaliated with a velvet threat: 'Gerard and I were giving tickets to *The Nutcracker* for a class outing, but now . . .'

Gerard, summoned out of a meeting at Kleinwort Gnome also rang Mrs Hornsby and said he understood the school needed a new computer, and he'd be happy to help, if only circumstances were different. It was indeed fortuitous that Tabitha Tollemache, the original Virgin Mary, was suddenly chosen as the youngest member of the school choir trip to Vienna. So now here they are: Gerard viewing his daughter entirely through his Sony digital camcorder. Pandora looks beatific; it's the quarter of valium her mother gave her so Panda might achieve the bovine serenity to pronounce, 'It's a boy.'

9

The Gap Year Student

IT WAS EXACTLY a year ago that the telephone trilled at Wallaby; it was Jamie's parents excitedly informing their old friend Rod that their son and heir had decided to spend his gap in Australia. Initially, the line seemed to go dead, and Jamie's father was left shouting into the echoes of long distance, 'I say, can you hear me, over?' Actually, the silence was due to Rod thinking, 'Not another idle Pommy git wet behind the ears from Eton,' but he reluctantly said he'd have Jamie on the sheep station. 'He'll have to muck in, mind, and there's no airs and graces at Wallaby.' So far, mucking-in has entailed Jamie enthusiastically driving 30 miles to the local pub for a few beers with the shearers. He was so trashed the next day, he didn't get out of bed until noon. 'Sorry, Rod, I must have caught the sun. Mummy says I should be really careful.' He's exceptionally careful to absent himself if there's any risk of dealing with the sheeps' bottoms. Rod's wife, Sally, who disembowelled Jamie's backpack when he and it arrived, smelling of dead rodents, says won't it be lovely when their Meggie is 18 and goes and stays with Jamie's parents in London?

Jamie gets a text message telling him there's an ace billet house-sitting in Sydney, stuffs his backpack and says magnanimously, 'If you're ever our way, Mummy would love to give you tea.' Once in Rose Bay, he chills by the pool and texts all his gap mates to meet him for a hooley in Paddo. The English population of Paddington is such that Jamie never has to tangle with an Australian. When his hostess returns home with the children and asks him to go and buy milk and bread, he says, 'Love to, but could you give me some cash? Ma and Pa are keeping me awfully short.' Which is presumably why he's drunk all the gin and tonic. As the BA flight takes off into Jamie's future at Edinburgh University, his Australian mentors resolve never again to answer the telephone in June.

'Not another idle Pommy git wet behind the ears from Eton'

The dogs, bitterly insecure, are using the florid family portrait of a hunting parson as a basket

The Couple Moving House

IN HER FRANTIC search for the corkscrew, Vanessa has so far unpacked a chicken brick, her collection of Georgette Heyer and four Pony Club ties. Martin has been poleaxed by the number of Herend ornaments they seem to possess and the dogs, bitterly insecure, are using the florid family portrait of a hunting parson as a basket. The little man who has come to erect the Ikea kitchen out of its flatpacks keeps popping his head round the door, saying, 'Any chance of a cuppa, luv? I'll swear I saw the kettle in the toilet.' Vanessa knows now that she has turned into Bridget Jones because, sans kitchen, her breakfast consisted of a ham and cheese sandwich with Branston pickle. Kind friends have sent champagne and a jasmine but active life is being sustained by pizza delivery. Vanessa feels her life has dwindled to ordering *quattro stagione* on her mobile, as BT have cut off the land line.

She profoundly wishes that the removal van had vanished between houses; she and Martin had agreed on no more clutter, yet it seems to have clung to them inexorably. Do they really need Martin's butterfly collection or her Carpenters albums? Yet every time she loads up a box for charity, Martin riffles through it and says, 'Don't chuck that out, Nessa, it might come in useful.' She snaps back that it's all very well, but they have nowhere to put the ironing board, let alone a pair of wooden elephants bought in Kensington Market. The vision of a pure Farrow & Ball off-white space is receding rapidly, although Nicky Haslam has wafted round and placed one sofa quite beautifully. Transfixed by the wall of packing cases, like a rabbit in the headlights, Vanessa doubts she will ever get to sit on it. She can only find one of her new Tod's loafers, the boiler has exploded and Martin inadvertently put the car keys in the fridge. Vanessa wants her mother.

The Sad Dad

NIGEL IS MAKING the cringey mistake of being conspiratorial with his daughter's friends. 'What ho, Tomkinson Minor, do I detect a whiff of the wicked weed behind your back? Let's play K.V. this time, I'll say nothing to your Mummy if you go and put it out in the shrubbery, like a good fellow.' God, how embarrassing is that? Davina is in tears in the loo because she think everyone thinks she's got a sad dad. Particularly after he made them all do Scottish dancing, and she so wanted her party to be cool. Nigel thinks cool is something to do with the weather. Davina begged for Barcardi Breezers and beer – 'All my friends have alcohol at their parties, Daddy' – but Nigel said his fruit cup was just the thing to make the party go wild, 'And we don't want it to go too wild, do we, Daffy Duck? Now, are you sure you don't want me to book that conjurer you used to enjoy so much?' Nigel said this in front of Minty Codrington. Davina hasn't been so humiliated since her father came to pick her up from the Feathers Ball, distinguishing himself from the mêlée of Range Rovers and blonde mothers by carrying a big balloon with 'Davina' written on it in magic marker. Then there was the time he played in the fathers' and daughters' tennis match in too-short shorts.

Nigel is cheerfully oblivious, turning up early to collect Davina from Minty's party and bumbling in to shake her friends by the hand, saying heartily, 'Hello. I'm Davina's father. Are you wicked ravers enjoying yourselves?' All the way home in the Toyota Previa, he teases Davina about pulling and snogging. 'Don't use our words, Dad, you don't know what they mean. And by the way, it's Glasstonbury, not Glastonbury, and I am going to go this year, whether you like it or not. And don't get cross with my friends, it's so flaky, particularly as everyone saw you kicking the car and shouting "Bollocks" when you had a puncture at the Carol Service.'

Nigel thinks cool is something to do with the weather

*Gideon is lethally proud of his talents as the daisy cutter of
projectile vomiting*

The New-Born Baby

HAVING BEEN SCANNED, monitored and had Mozart played to him to make him more intelligent, Gideon arrived in a birthing pool. It is not what he would have chosen – a Caesarean would have been less stressful, not to mention more dignified – and he has screamed furiously ever since, wails of Machiavellian anguish entirely disproportionate to his 5lb 8oz. His mother is now a sobbing wreck, her torrential condition exacerbated by hay fever from the flowers sent by excited girlfriends: 'Congratulations! We never knew you had it in you!' Granny (who doesn't want to be called Granny – 'I'm far too young, darling') is on the gin. Only the maternity nurse, an ace dragon, has got Gideon's measure. The stern crackle of her starched bosom above the cot transforms the vociferous, wrinkled crab apple within to Nursie's cooing, gurgly little plum. Gideon can recognise an expert when he sees one. Nursie warms her hands before changing his nappy; the Mummy person is frankly a liability with the nappy pin, and Gideon didn't like Daddy's tone when he said that just because some fathers might be dab hands on the changing mat, that didn't mean every chap had to do it. And Granny's breath smells funny. Only last night she made Mummy even more hysterical by saying she didn't know why Gideon's presence had reduced the entire house to Plastic World. While Gideon may lack comprehension, he's exquisitely sensitive to innuendo. It will take him some time to dissociate Uncle Rupert from the unpleasant words he used after falling over the pram in the hall. Only Nursie is consistently reliable. Gideon likes routine, and cosy bottles with Nursie in the night. Mummy says breast is best, but there was the terrible night she ate curry, and Gideon exploded conclusively at both ends. He is lethally proud of his talents as the daisy cutter of projectile vomiting. Everyone tiptoes round the house saying 'Ssshh . . . Don't do anything to upset Gideon.'

The Couple at the Gym

Gloria and Ted have thrust the Gordon's to the back of the drinks cupboard and joined the gym. Ted finds balancing his bottom on a rubber exercise ball shamingly difficult and has fallen off repeatedly, his spindly legs flailing out of his old tennis shorts. Neither Ted nor Gloria has grasped the fashion dynamic of the Bright Lite Health Club; Gloria unearthed the leotard she last wore when she was going for the burn with Jane Fonda. It now has a slightly grey tinge and her poly-cotton T-shirt clings to her in an extravaganza of wrinkly droop. Ted reluctantly bought new trainers – 'Trainers! Ridiculous word. Whatever's wrong with plimsolls?' – at the Bright Lite Rite-On sports shop because the soles had rotted on his Dunlop Green Flashes. Gloria, pumping weights into the air with grisly determination, has mistaken a Day-glo headband for the Elle Macpherson look, particularly unattractive when combined with the fury engendered by giving up smoking.

By day three Gloria has decided that it would be less stressy to do it gradually, thus allowing herself a teeny-weeny Silk Cut to alleviate the tedium of still mineral water and lettuce at supper. By day 10 Ted has inexorably crept up on the drinks cupboard. It cannot be right that the Gordon's bottle should remain all alone in the dark. He absolves his conscience with low-cal tonic. It is filthy, so must be good for him, but necessitates a lot more gin to drown the taste. A chap has to have a bit of leeway, particularly after the shock of losing concentration on the treadmill and finding himself splatted against the wall. Gloria joins yoga for beginners, also pilates and ayurvedic meditation, like an indiscriminate fresher at university. Her new best friend Carole – met in acupuncture – gets her to sign up for reflexology. As Ted dumps the offending trainers into the oblivion of the dog room, Gloria is forging a new life at the rockface of alternative therapy.

*Neither Ted nor Gloria has quite grasped the fashion dynamic of the
Bright Lite Healthclub*

'Mirror, mirror, mirror,' he says. 'You cannot overdo the mirror, Sophie.'

The Driving Instructor

ERIC HAS FLUID wrist movements from demonstrating the manual hand signal, arm extended out of the car window. This balletic gesture, together with the thump of his foot on to the dual controls in an involuntary braking motion, constitutes his sole exercise in a sedentary job fraught with disappointment. Mrs Budge just simply won't when it comes to reverse; young Sophie – now she's a one – always fails to get the handbrake on at the penultimate movement of the three-point turn. 'Mirror, mirror, mirror,' he says to her. 'You cannot overdo the mirror, Sophie.' And she quite agrees, because the mirror is really handy for checking her lipgloss. There are times when Eric goes home and confides to his tropical fish that women are hopeless, only outdone in dangerous volatility by young men who think that they know everything and have no reverence for the stop-handbrake-first-gear-move-off-slowly principles of responsible motoring. 'Secure the car' is what Eric is constantly telling Rupert Skivington, but there was an unfortunate incident when a row of traffic cones was bowled over like skittles because Rupert's mobile rang in the midst of a parallel manoeuvre. It gave Eric quite a turn. 'The examiner won't like that,' he says reedily as Rupert rasps round a deceptive corner. Eric knows that within seconds of passing his test Rupert will be driving an automatic BMW convertible. He vents the unfairness of it all on the beauteous socialite Barbie White, who has had to undergo 50 hours' tuition despite holding a Canadian licence. Eric has shown his wife her photograph in *Hello!* but stoutly refrains from complimenting a colonial on her mastery of 'live traffic' in Kensington. He was doing 'mirror, mirror, mirror' with her when she vehemently questioned whether he expected her neck to have the flexibility of a Balinese dancer. No one ever spoke like that to Eric when he was in the Army catering corps.

21

The Elderly Swimmer

LEONIE LUDGROVE SWIMS every morning at the Chelsea Baths. They may be public, but they are within the Royal borough. She is appalled at the idea of paying some newfangled health club for the privilege of doing 25 lengths of breaststroke in a swimming-pool with Mozart piped underwater. What on earth would be the point when one never puts one's head in? Her progress through the water is that of a periscope disguised as a purple chrysanthemum in her Peter Jones swimming cap, head held firmly in the air on the swan-like neck of exquisite breeding. In case of inadvertent facial contact with anything wet, Lady Ludgrove had her eyebrows tattooed at Harrods. It would never do to have streaky eye pencil when buying skinless chicken breasts for the peke in Waitrose on the way home. She always walks, of course; she prides herself on her lithe, youthful suppleness. Leonie Ludgrove can still touch her toes. Sir Horace, who dotes, and whose vision of her is further enhanced by the soft-focus of failing eyesight, says she's a mere girl. In the winter they go to La Mamounia, renowned for its exceptionally large pool, and Sir Horace reads military history under a sun umbrella while she glides by, occasionally stopping to tread water beside him and ask, 'Is it time for your pills, dear?'

Back in Chelsea Baths, her young friend Chloe (a single mother, but a nice person nevertheless) admires Lady Ludgrove's light tan. That night, while cleansing vigorously with Pond's Cold Cream, Leonie tells Horace that one meets some charming people in the slow lane. Their son offered to make her a member of the Berkeley Health Club and Spa ('Have a few treatments, Mummy – stop you whiffing of chlorine, eh?') but Lady Ludgrove thought the pool very small – no good for laps whatsoever and, besides, it might be full of foreigners. No, these modern places come and go but the Chelsea Baths have been there since 1907.

*Lady Ludgrove's progress through the water is that of a
periscope disguised as a purple chrysanthemum in her Peter Jones
swimming cap*

Sir Reginald is not entirely sure he hasn't got a touch of malaria;
a G&T might be just the thing – because of the quinine,
don't ya know

The Ambassadorial Couple

SIR REGINALD FEATHERWIT is a disappointed man. He had always seen himself in Washington or Paris, or at a push, Rome, and here he is in Zarovia. The plumbing in the embassy regurgitates, the mosquitoes are indestructible and the natives damn tricky. There isn't a day that passes without these chaps coming along with land issues and mineral rights. Frankly, Sir Reginald is sick of it, and not entirely sure he hasn't got a touch of malaria. A gin and tonic might be just the thing – because of the quinine, don't ya know. Lady Featherwit gently reminds him about the Zarovian Ladies' Harp Circle Gala and he roars that he cannot be expected to conduct delicate diplomatic negotiations if he has to go and listen to a lot of harpies. And must they have a mulligatawny soup again for lunch? Doesn't the wretched chef know how to cook anything else? 'Honestly, Rosalie, I would have thought you could get some of Deirdre Smith's books out in the diplomatic bag and show Tuppence a thing or two. Nice enough fellow, trying hard, but get him some recipes that have nothing to do with goats. His goat gets my gout.' Lady Featherwit smiles her bright, watery smile and says, 'Certainly, dear,' in much the same way as she will say, 'How frightfully nice of you to come,' and 'Aren't the hydrangeas something?' at the garden party.

Sometimes her armour of paisley floral and mummy's pearls is not enough to make her feel completely like the dear, late Queen Mother, but she aspires. 'Reginald is delighted that you have come, Chief Tsaranoro, we regard you as such a special guest. And how is your charming wife after the happy event? That will be your 15th son, I understand. I must say that Sir Reginald and I both come from large families – although not quite so large in Norfolk – and it has been a joy.' At night, she says, 'Reggie? Do try not to be so cross, darling, you're doing it for Great Britain PLC.'

The Software Designer

STEWART IS DEVELOPING Pop Icon, the new game for Mega. It's going to be bigger than Tetris, sexier than Tomb Raider, more violent than Grand Theft Auto 3 on Playstation 2. Virtual blood will be spilt in the contest to become a pop heartthrob, circumnavigating hazards such as wearing glittery platform shoes and singing *Dancing Queen*. Stewart is currently working on the 3D graphics, and inputting millions of lines of code. It was for this that he achieved his first-class degree in mathematics at Cambridge: to become the priest of a modern-day sect, decoding the liturgy of ones and zeros. Buffy the Vampire Slayer is his Mary Magdalen; a creature from *Monsters Inc* tucked furrily among the congealed coffee cups is his conceptual inspiration. When Stewart looks entirely blank, his sausagey fingers flying across the keyboard, he has gone into the zone – a deep meditative state of coding. At moments of high excitement, when he's found a showstopper bug, Stewart removes his shoes, a reflex of searing aromatic intensity. An entire eco-system lives in his sweater, fuelled by pizza droppings. The convivial niceties of social eating have been obscured by his hyper-intelligent analytical creative skills. This is a man who names his servers Princess Leia, Gandalf and Han Solo; who speaks the language of bytes and glitches; *PC Format* constitutes a tottering tower in his bedroom.

Stewart may not possess deodorant, but he is blessed with cryptic insight into the brave new world of electronic superiority. If Stewart says Intergalactic Sword & Sorcery is 'pants', then it's no-good rubbish; the designers should go back to playing Command and Conquer. The only way to demystify Stewart's terrifying modern wizardry is to regard him as plumber, for when you show him your system, he always sucks his teeth and says 'Who did this then? I'll have to build you a new one.'

Stewart has gone into the zone – a deep meditative state of coding

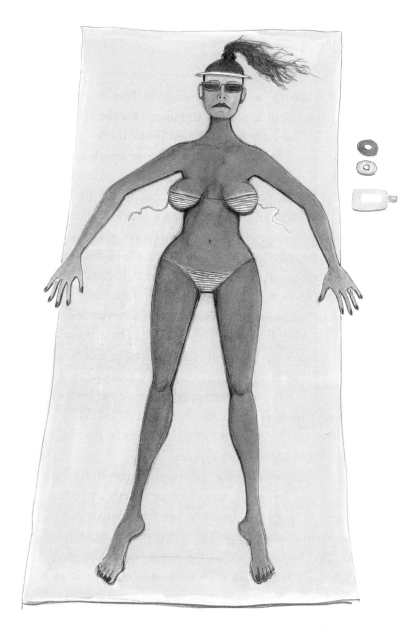

She has to lie spreadeagled, fingers rigidly apart, so the sun can kiss every oiled crevice

The Obsessive Tanner

KARINA HAD ST TROPEZ before she went to St Tropez. She flogged down to a marvellous little woman in Fulham for the last appointment of the day. There she was slathered in the thinking woman's fake tan and gingerly returned home to sleep on towels so as not to stain her Frette sheets with orange skid marks. Auto-bronzed, waxed, exfoliated and pedicured, Karina can appear for lunch at Club 55 without fear, but only stays for the crudités. Lunch takes up valuable tanning time. Fortified by two pieces of broccoli and a dab of anchoiade, she returns to the beach to broil flesh anointed with Clarins Bronzage Rapide. She cannot read, because a Danielle Steele would cast a shadow on her cleavage, and she has to lie spreadeagled, fingers rigidly apart, so the sun can kiss every oiled crevice. The only acceptable tide marks are those defined by diamond rings. So there is the requisite, exquisitely uncomfortable, half hour lying on each side to achieve all-round colour, like a chicken on a spit, and of course the contortions necessary to release her bikini top so the strap doesn't leave a mark across her back. At breakfast, before anyone else gets up, she prostrates herself topless by the villa's pool with cotton wool pads over her nipples.

When everyone goes out on a day trip to Avignon, Karina has a little headache and says she'll 'stay at home quietly', which means that she'll get the pool boy to rotate her sun lounger in order to receive consistently full-on rays. This will make the nightclub debut of her white Prada dress as impactful as if it were worn by Naomi Campbell in les Caves du Roy (Karina only comes out at night when the sun is in). A day away from St Tropez and she has booked at Fantasy Tan, the exciting equivalent of putting her body through a spray-paint job. It may be the only bulwark against her future as a crocodile handbag.

*Evie and Grace regard champagne as a non-alcoholic drink of which
there should be a great deal*

The Annual Party Givers

EVIE AND GRACE have had their New Year's Day drinks party ever since Colonel Pettigrew, Grace's husband, died and thus ceased to complain about damn strangers darkening the doorstep of The Grange, hosing back his Amontillado. 'It's just a little gathering,' says Evie. 'To cheer up January,' says Grace. 'Do bring your house party,' says Evie. 'We love to see the young,' says Grace. The young, deep-rooted in the sofa with *EastEnders* and thumping hangovers, groan and beg, 'Do we have to go to the old ducks, Mum?' and then find themselves having rather a good time. They hadn't seen the Huntlys all Christmas, and – wow – Minnie Huntly's grown into a right little smasher. Evie does a riproaring Bloody Mary; Grace says a party isn't a party without White Ladies, and both regard champagne as a non-alcoholic drink of which there should be a great deal. The sisters fluttered with pleasurable anxiety during the preparations – did they have enough chipolatas, and perhaps a discreet bucket might be a good idea in the conservatory, where Sophia Lumsden was sick last year. Dear Sophia, she must have had that nasty bug that was going round. The Tomkinsons, who met at Evie's and Grace's party, what a happy day that was, are bringing their new twins and their new puppy. The twins will be best in the yellow bedroom, the puppy in the gun room, so splendid to have a use for it since Colonel Pettigrew's demise. Flippy Titmarsh has bearded Max Hastings in the hall; the celebrated house guests of others illuminate the sisters with pleasure (such fun when the Osbornes brought Clare Francis) but Grace, having been a colonel's wife, is skilled at extricating them from bores. And gently ousting Blinker Huntly from under the mistletoe, so he can't pinch all the girls' bottoms, demanding a kiss. 'Aren't Evie and Grace absolutely wonderful?' says everyone as they purr down the drive. 'We must have them over.' But they never do.

Evelyn is knitting a scarf made of Pekingese combings

The Dog Handler

EVELYN CREATES A homely little oasis on the film set. While all about her are in black singlets, Evelyn is vivid in Crimplene, knitting furiously in a fug of hot tea and damp dog, Twinkle having been freshly bathed for his next take with Helena Bonham Carter. It is very important that Twinkle doesn't get stressed; there was no end of trouble on *102 Dalmatians* because the puppies got so over-excited that they then fell asleep at the critical moment. Repeat puppies had to be sent for, and you could never repeat Twinkle. He is a dog of charm and sound temperament, and has been an angel with Miss Bonham Carter, following her devotedly. (Evelyn gave a teeny hint to wardrobe about sewing choc drops into Helena's crinoline.) It seems unimaginable that Pip the terrier was preferred for the role alongside Michael Gambon in *Gosford Park*. Evelyn had to have a medicinal whisky to get over the shock – when she got home to Egham, of course; she takes no risks driving the dogs. The Volvo, with its back seat down so they have plenty of room, is a mobile kennel with squashy tartan dog beds, little bowls of biccie and the chewed relics of old Smackos wedged under the gearstick.

When she opens the boot there is a pungent aroma of dog breath, Pedigree Chum and her knitting – for she is working on a scarf made of Pekingese combings: 'The new pashmina, Evelyn, or should I say Pekinina?' says the director, standing respectfully upwind. Having got Twinkle ready for his close-up, she settles down with a copy of *Dog News*. Anyone aspiring to chat her up has only to ask, 'How's the family, Evelyn?' to unleash a flood of information about Twinkle's walkies and the Nobel intelligence required to sit, beg and jump on cue. 'We have worked with Dame Judi Dench,' she says conclusively. The script supervisor was put firmly in her place. 'Why is Twinkle called Twinkle, Evelyn?' 'Because he's a star, dear.'

The Sponger

JIMMY OLIPHANT ARRIVES for the weekend with a very small box of chocolates, most of which he will eat himself. He has invited himself to stay, having caught Kitty Cavendish on the hop between coping with the cat's hairballs and doing the Sainsbury's shop. 'Kitty? Little one? I wonder what you and Charles are doing Friday to Sunday?' And because the question could not hang interminably in the air, since Kitty needed to ring the vet, she gave in. 'Oh, we're not doing anything much. Would you like to come down? Kitchen sups on Saturday.' Charles was livid. 'Bloody man. Smokes all my cigars. Absolute girl in the bathroom. Last time he used all the hot water, and he's got that frightful little hairdresser's car.'

The next thing the Cavendishes know, a Japanese Dinky toy crunches up their gravel and Jimmy is shimmering on the doorstep. 'Heeello,' he says, in an eerie approximation of Terry-Thomas. His teeth are all mossy because he's too mean to go to the dental hygienist, and the Heseltine hair irritates Charles (who's thinning) even more than Jimmy slapping him on the back saying, 'Wonderful to see you, maestro,' or Jimmy's cufflinks adorned with the regimental crest. 'Insufferable prat. He only did a short-service commission and he's still going round calling himself Captain.'

It was only the other day that, during a robust lunch at White's, Oily Oliphant's name came up in the chat and at least four chaps recalled that he'd been one of their ushers, but had never given them a wedding present. By the end of the weekend, even though Jimmy has sugared her with inconsequential charm, Kitty is thoroughly exasperated. He leaves £1.80 beside the bed for the maid – with which, having washed his clothes and helped him to pack, she descends the stairs and says, with dignity, 'Captain Oliphant, I think you have left something behind.' And Oily trousers it.

*His teeth are all mossy because he's too mean to go to
the dental hygienist*

The Raconteur's Wife

TESSA HAS HEARD them all before, particularly the one about the time Roger was Whizzer Fancott's best man and they went to the wrong church. 'Lots of people Whizzer knew there, glad-handed most of the congregation going up the aisle, only realised there was an almighty muddle when the real bridegroom arrived. Made our excuses and left, and Whizzer had to manhandle the bride out of her car – damn lucky she wasn't his, I swear she had a wart – in order to palm the driver 20 quid to get us to the right church on time.' This always goes down well at weddings, and Tessa smiles and laughs in the right places because it is the way Roger tells them, and he's a dear old love, and at least he doesn't tell jokes about Englishmen, Irishmen and Scotsmen. Some of the stories have acquired a rich cadence and the patina of embellishment: the time he got stuck in a lift with Margaret Thatcher – 'And lived!' – and when he chaired a literary lunch for the grandes dames of romantic fiction and Catherine Cookson confided to Barbara Cartland that she'd just finished her 40th book, and Barbara Cartland said that was a mere bagatelle, she'd written her 396th oeuvre. 'To which Catherine Cookson retorted smartly, "Really, Barbara dear? I didn't know you wrote one every year."'

Although Tessa sometimes relies upon champagne to get her through the longer anecdotes, she has never spoilt a punchline in 20 years of marriage, nor seeks to hijack the audience's attention with tales of her children's gap-year exploits. She has long since resigned herself to an adoring silence, at best a one-woman Greek chorus occasionally moving Roger's plot forward if he appears to be losing it. 'Wonderfully amusing fellow, your husband,' strangers say admiringly, and Tessa nods appreciatively and tries not to think about the times at home, with no audience, when Roger hardly speaks to her at all.

Tessa has never spoilt a punchline in 20 years of marriage

The Food Allergy Sufferer

DAMIEN SWEARS BY Dr Chong. It was while holding one of Dr Chong's little metal bars in his left hand, and rotating his arm anticlockwise, that they discovered Damien was allergic to wheat and dairy. Pasta is now forbidden fruit to him, he can have only the merest smidgen of semi-skimmed in his decaffeinated filter coffee, of which he allows himself only one cup, having truly switched to green tea. But one must have one's little vices – a decaffeinated a day keeps the diet bore away, is what Damien tells his fellow graphic designers, while waving a hand emphatically in front of their cigarette smoke. If he is being really racy he might have a half-and-half with dinner (half Evian and half Badoit). Dr Chong has said he shouldn't touch alcohol – the sugar will give him false highs – and shellfish must be treated with caution, Damien is acutely nervous that one prawn will inflate him into the Hindenburg.

He goes for patch tests for new and more exciting allergies at Farmacia every Saturday, and steams the vegetables he buys at Planet Organic with mineral water because there's so much progesterone in recycled tap water from women taking the Pill, he's frightened he might grow breasts. He is also trying to eat right for his blood type. This means that when invited to dinner he has to wave away pork with crackling (fat – years might be wiped off his heart), beef, duck, garlic, tomatoes and anything with oil. 'Do forgive me, it is because I am an O group. Oh no, not the bread, thank you, carbohydrate induces food coma. I'll just have a little undressed rocket salad and a rice cake.' Scrambled egg? How very kind, but does his hostess personally know the hens who laid the eggs? Damien may wonder why he spends so many evenings alone with a wheatgrass vitamin shake, Dr Chong's version of liquid lawn.

If he is being really racy he might have a half-and-half with dinner (half Evian and half Badoit)

The contorted willow got caught in Lord Woolpit's hearing aid

The Party Waitress

LAURETTE HAS POSITIVELY sculptural forearms from manipulating Palladian fantasies of canapés through parties of people too fashionable to eat. All In Good Taste Ltd currently espouses cartouches of reconstituted stone on which three quail's eggs and a seashell of celery salt are balanced amid ornamental cabbages, bamboo and contorted willow. They weigh a ton, and at a private view of the Van Dyck exhibition the contorted willow got caught in Lord Woolpit's hearing aid. All In Good Taste reverted temporarily to glass platters full of grey pebbles from which it was very difficult to distinguish the caviare blinis.

Ironing her white blouse and black M&S skirt, Laurette wonders why she does this job. The answer is £7 an hour while she pays off her student loan. Her mother says that it is very good experience, and that Laurette might meet a nice young man at one of these grand parties. Laurette thinks this is extremely unlikely, given that guests either treat the waitresses as invisible ambulatory buffets, or limit conversation to a bright inquisition about the mini quiches. 'Heavens, those look delicious – now what *are* they? Roasted vegetables with fresh pesto. Whatever will they think of next? No I won't, thanks awfully.' And Laurette is waved away with her flower vase stuffed with rosebuds on which the offending quiches are balanced on a window pane. Laurette has learnt a great deal about people's eating habits: sandwiches are social arsenic, women only ever take the prawns (no mayonnaise) and men only eat when the women aren't looking. The pink, sweaty property dealers wink at her conspiratorially if caught taking a second miniaturised cone of fish and chips wrapped in the *FT*. Laurette smiles back politely, thinking all the while of a hot bath, *Friends* and buying support tights before the Sudeleys' bash at Spencer House.

The Economy-Class Passenger

NOTHING IN HEATHER's experience of living in Shropshire has prepared her for sleeping with total strangers. It is over Pakistan that the Australian in the window seat consumes his fourth tin of Fosters, belches contentedly and lolls on to her shoulder. Fatso on the aisle seat is overflowing her arm rest. It is going to be a long way to Sydney; Heather's legs are encased in anti-DVT socks with the grip of a boa constrictor. She is wearing loose clothing, as advised, but was so depressed by the idea of tracksuit bottoms that she bought drawstring cashmere trousers which cost nearly a third of the air fare. Then there is the pashmina to replace the airline blanket with its horrid chemical smell, and the herbal sleeping pills and extra-strength moisturiser. Honestly, she might just as well have thrust the cost of these dignified style statements towards a Club Class ticket.

Heather wants to watch a movie, but the man in front reclines with a mighty bounce, ramming the seat-back TV into her meal tray. It is at this point that she nearly begs to have the drinks trolley applied intravenously, if only she were confident of subsequently mountaineering over Fatso's prone form to get to the loo. After Singapore her teeth feel all furry, as if they are wearing little coats. The baby in the next row is screaming, its mother looking defiant as the child-hardened weary around her unite in a unanimous think bubble of Calpol. The toddler behind Heather kicks her continually from 30,000 ft over Perth. At the journey's end, as she is liberating her Melbourne Cup hat, the toddler's father says, 'It's people like you what ought to buy your own aeroplane', and Heather says, 'Believe me, sir, I am now going to work on it.'

Heather begs to have the drinks trolley applied intravenously

*Claudine really cannot be bothered to explain to pygmy intellects
about submerging meaning in a material anxiety of significance*

The Modern Art Curator

CLAUDINE VERHOEVEN CONSIDERS that exhibitions are about ideas – hers – and the artists should strive to interpret the purity of the concept with no subversive individualism. What she wants is a heaving white mass of moribund, ideological pathos where transcendent longing struggles with dystopian entropy. Hans Frenzi, a favourite for the Turnip Prize, has achieved her minimalist dictates filtered through a lugubrious romanticism. Each evening, when the public have left, Claudine stomps down to the Driffield Galleries of Vision UK and thinks how perfectly exquisite Frenzi's theatrically stylised obelisks are, set off by the tiny brown fossilised dog turd and lit with a naked 40w bulb. The critics do not appreciate it – frightful little people with beards (Claudine is oblivious to her own moustache, an unwaxed totem of feminist defiance), and the public are an ignorant maelstrom of students and tweedy old women saying, 'Well, Daphne, I don't call this art, do you?'

Claudine really cannot be bothered to explain to pygmy intellects about submerging meaning in a material anxiety of significance. Her protégé, Frank Dracona, won the Philbossian Award for his eliptical work on this theme with a bubble machine and three metronomes. Claudine particularly espouses artists who work with music, air, light or text to create multimedia experiences playfully preoccupied with the conundrum of significance and nullity. Others at art gallery soirées feel as if they have been beaten around the head by her intellect and revealed as intellectual minnows. 'She collects for Charles Scorsese, don'tcha know?' Immediately everyone appreciates Claudine Verhoeven's acute visual sensitivity, her sense of actuality or space and her personal anxiety – as described in her foreword to the catalogue – about 'making something extra, that is simultaneously something and nothing for the world'.

The Home Tutor

SEBASTIAN IS BORED. He achieved his double first at Oxford with casual brilliance and is shortly starting work at Goldman Sachs, but meanwhile he is trying to drum Keats into the soggy lump of rice pudding sitting beside him. He needs the money for a trip to Leptis Magna in Libya, to study Hadrianic Roman baths with an archaeologist from the British Museum. This is the sort of thing he does for amusement, while Becky's ideas of creative leisure are confined to the King's Road. Thus they are not twin souls. Sebastian would rather be writing his novel, and Becky has seen some really wicked lavender nail varnish in Mac. He wonders if it's because she's so lumpy that she is so unpoetical. She wonders if Sebastian has chosen Keats because he is trying to say something wildly romantic to her. All her friends think he's cool in his fleece and his Timberlands. Lisa Lacey says his hair is soooo Byronic. Since Becky has such a tenuous relationship with Eng Lit, which is why she's having the coaching, this reference is lost on her, but she thinks it sounds good. Personally, she sees him as Matthew Broderick, with herself as Reese Witherspoon, in *Election*.

Thankfully unaware of the fantasy video in Becky's head, Sebastian bids her to concentrate on *Endymion*. Her reading of the verse is such an acutely painful experience that she actually commands his undivided attention. 'Well, Becky,' he says faintly, 'I think we certainly deserve a cup of coffee after that.' The prospect of having to tackle Gerard Manley Hopkins, whose art is dependent upon cadence, looms next week. Fortunately he'll be spared, or rather summarily dismissed by Becky's mother, who is about to discover her daughter's torrid diary of Sebastian's Byronic activities. Written with spirited input from Lisa Lacey, it is a more imaginative work of fiction than Sebastian's novel.

Sebastian is trying to drum Keats into the soggy lump of rice pudding sitting beside him

The Hen Night

NIKKI THINKS ELVIS the Pelvis is a right laugh. Amy from Accounts (who's posh because her father's a barrister) wanted the girls to have a refined spa experience: manicures and pedicures at Nails 'R' Us, with dry white wine and balsamic vinegar Kettle Chips, but Cheryl said, 'Get a life, Ames, this is Nikki's last night of wicked wanton debauchery, we're all going to the Sex and the City karaoke bar.' So they have, and Cheryl has just ordered a third round of neon pink Satin Seductions – although Amy said she'd prefer a Perrier. Buoyant with the seductive qualities of vodka mixed with Campari, strawberry ice-cream and sugar-cane syrup, Nikki is going for it. Her wedding is two weeks away, and Gary, her intended, is in Paris with his mates watching the rugby.

Cheryl and Debra did suggest they all flew Virgin to Las Vegas for a Hen Weekend ('Virgin, geddit Nikki?') but Jackie couldn't afford the flight and Amy didn't know what to wear, and Nikki said she'd bet Elvis the Pelvis up the West End was better than anything in Vegas. She's read about him in *Time Out* and now here he is, a pulsating amalgam of muscle and Mantan. Amy is so startled she's downed Cheryl's Satin Seduction in one gulp. It's so awfully good that she drinks another. Nikki says Gary will look just like Elvis the Pelvis when he's on the beach during their honeymoon in Mykonos. She wins the karaoke competition singing *Stand By Your Man* and at 1am they all wobble home to her flat in a minicab and make spag bol. Amy, now on the red wine, says she 'wants a man like Pelvis the Elvis, but with hist here' and has to make a determined rush at the words to formulate 'chest hair'. Who would have thought Amy had a thing about chest hair? Later, Nikki holds Amy's head while she's sick in the lav, and everyone watches a video of the bit in *Four Weddings and a Funeral* when Wet Wet Wet sing *Love is All Around*.

Cheryl has just ordered a third round of neon pink Satin Seductions

The Newly Retired Husband

ANDREW IS ECSTATIC about his early retirement. He is going to spend more time with his garden, catalogue the library and make prawns wrapped in filo pastry – it looked marvellously easy on *Ready, Steady, Cook*. Angela is boiling with rage. The sound principle of marrying for life, but not for lunch, was also supposed to embrace breakfast, which Andrew now wants in its entirety, even going so far as grilled mushrooms. Angela tried attrition, but if no breakfast is forthcoming, Andrew pointedly makes toast at 11am, so the whole house smells and there are crumbs all over the Aga. 'Don't worry about me, darling,' he says, 'I can look after myself.' Thus he's always popping into her study to ask where the Marmite is, and why no one seems to have got more tonic water. She sent him off to Tesco in Winchester, which was fatal because he came back with lots of things not on the list, and was so shattered by the expense that he demanded to see the household bills for the first time in 25 years. Now he goes round the house turning off all the lights to save electricity.

When Angela has her girls' bridge afternoon, she turfs Andrew out to the pub to have lunch with Colonel Carberry, but when he returns he looks at her hand and says, with beery breath, 'If you'd led another trump, you'd have made another trick.' It's almost as irritating as the fact that he keeps on answering the telephone, hitherto Angela's sole preserve. And every time she wants to listen to *The Archers*, it's crackle, crackle, crackle because Andrew has retuned her Roberts radio to get the Test match. He has discovered B&Q, and bought an enormous amount of DIY equipment with which to re-hang the pictures in the dining-room, a project foiled when he put a six-inch nail through the hot-water pipe. He will have far too much time on his hands to get round to cataloguing the library.

Andrew is always popping into Angela's study to ask where the Marmite is

Her French manicure has never experienced the rough and tumble of the flowerbed

The Flirt

SERENA HAS PERFECTED the breathy whisper of confidences, the light touch on a man's arm which makes him tingle, as her Jo Malone Red Rose – so simple, so heady – wafts around him. Serena never talks of school fees or property prices, but asks, 'Are you happy?' which flatteringly implies that Roderick has an emotional life, something which other women, knowing that he is married, correctly surmise he does not. 'When I heard I was sitting next to you at dinner, I was quite overawed,' she says shyly, her eyes cerulean blue with contact lenses. 'Running the Deutsche Gremlin Bank must be so exciting.' Roderick's eyes pop wetly as Serena leans towards him. Her talents, loosely defined as being an interior decorator, are actually in research. She always calls her hosts and asks, in a gentle, intimate way which conceals the extreme rudeness, who will be at the party. Then she bones up on the interesting ones; she's assiduously cultivated journalist friends who will fax her the cuttings. Men, accustomed to sitting next to women with little patches of baby sick on their shoulders, are entranced as Serena gazes at them from under broad-brimmed lashes, her skin polished with Eau Dynamisante. Her pashmina, wrap-lined with sheared mink – even the hottest June day can be so treacherous – would probably fund wee Hamish's entire term at Ludgrove. Her French manicure has never experienced the rough and tumble of the flowerbed, nor can Serena remember when she last washed her own hair. 'You obviously have such a rich inner life. I, too, become starved without books – it's so difficult to find any in the Hamptons,' she confides. What a stressful life this frail creature has; Roderick is only slightly disenchanted when, come the second course, he hears Serena having exactly the same conversation with the man on her left.

The Bridge Players

CORA BRACEGIRDLE IS steaming. Her partner has led an ace on which her king is going to fall, and her eyes are saying it with thunderbolts across the green baize. Giles Peabrayne is exceedingly pleased with himself, but has quite thrown away the trick; what is more, he spent aeons rapt in thought before pulling out this devastatingly wrong card. The late Colonel Bracegirdle always said, 'If you can't play well, play fast', and now this damn fool has thwarted his grieving widow's chances of savaging Enid and Violet Dodsworth with a grand slam doubled. And Mrs Bracegirdle thought they had it on toast.

It is indeed a severe caution against putting one's trust in a man who says he's been taking bridge lessons. Giles should have known better than to talk so flagrantly about the Stayman convention over the salmon; no such London cleverness could outflank Mrs Bracegirdle's technique, hardened in the dowager's bridge four on Thursdays.

Violet Dodsworth's pearls are heaving upon her bosom in anticipation of the post-mortem she will enjoy with Enid on their way home in the Rover, every card remembered and mulched over.

Evenings with dear Cora are such an excitement, fuelled by gin and the frisson of playing for 10p a hundred. 'My mother lived to the age of 96 on gin and bridge and I have every intention of doing the same,' says Mrs Bracegirdle, who engaged her butler, Totteridge, purely because he could mix white ladies and make up a four in extremis on wet afternoons. Perfectly steady player, Totteridge, no aggressive overcalling, capable of a successful finesse, unlike this pilchard smirking opposite her. Any moment now the fish-dished dunce will be fooling around not drawing trumps, or 'walking the Embankment'. At this particular moment Mrs Bracegirdle would like to push him over it.

'If you can't play well, play fast'

*Home, with its smells of toast and roast chicken, is being left behind
for the greater good of the dorm*

The Prep School Farewell

IT HAS BEEN a silent car journey to Ludgrove, Lorna sitting beside a complete stranger in stiff clean clothes, with scrubbed freckles and a savage haircut. She's occasionally said bright, inconsequential things such as 'There's not much traffic – we're awfully lucky, Whiskers', and Archie has squirmed in his seatbelt because this is the road to leaving childhood nicknames behind. Neither has dared to talk about home, because that whole warm, lamp-lit world, with its smells of toast and roast chicken, is being left behind for the greater good of the dorm. 'It's going to be such fun,' says Lorna desperately, wondering if she's sewn the nametapes on Archie's rugby shirts correctly. Her palms are sweating in case they get to school too early, looking like eager beavers, or too late so she is classified as a slacker mother. Arriving in the melée of BMWs, Archie looks dwarfed and is swallowed by the building; it was a humiliating mistake to buy his trousers 'to last' because they are wrinkling round his ankles; the dormitory is like Colditz. Lorna's heart breaks so violently she thinks Archie must hear it as he hugs her saying, 'Don't worry, Mum, I'll see you in two weeks.' As she leaves he trots off to swap gobstoppers with Alexander Pomeroy.

Lorna heads blindly down the drive and stops in the nearest layby, where, along with three other new mothers in steamed-up cars, she sobs on the steering wheel, blowing her nose on an escapee nametaped sock. At home, she sits in Archie's hollow, empty bedroom where the faint smell of pongy trainers is now more precious than Chanel No 5. Each morning she waits for the postman with an anticipation last accorded to a teenage crush. Finally the letter arrives: 'Dear Mum and Dad, I hope you are well. I am well. Chelsea won two-nil yesterday and we beat Summerfields at rugby. Longing to see you next Saturday and please bring lots of tuck.'

*Martin's sandals are only slightly less offensive to Lady Fossle
than his pink Aids ribbon*

The Politically Correct
Vicar

MARTIN UPSET THE entire village when he told the schoolchildren that Father Christmas did not exist. All the six-year-olds were reduced to tears and Lady Fossle confronted the wretched man in the vicarage. He explained, in tones of lugubrious self-righteousness that put her dentures on edge, that Father Christmas is an untruth and sexist. Lady Fossle said with asperity that Father Christmas had never done anybody any harm, unlike Mr Bin Liner for whom Martin had had the impertinence to offer prayers in the spirit of forgiveness. Martin wrung his hands moistly and said forgiveness was the greatest of human virtues and that the events of September 11 must inspire the congregation of St John's with an openness to all faiths and attitudes. Lady Fossle snorted and said that what the congregation of St John's needed as inspiration was Onward Christian Soldiers, which Martin had notably omitted on Remembrance Sunday. Nor did he allow the veterans their parade to church, on the grounds that it might upset German residents. Germans in Upton Lacey are confined to Mrs Stoddart's au pair, but Martin came from an inner-city parish and is haunted by the plight of immigrants and refugees. He is concerned that Tony Blair has little compassion for the inner city, and nurtures secret approval of the Prince of Wales's work for urban regeneration, which sits uncomfortably with his conviction that the Royal Family are leeches on society. Over their vegetarian supper, Martin and his wife Marion (a teacher) debate the ideological quandary of praying for the Queen in matins. It makes Martin's toes curl in his Birkenstocks – an item of apparel only slightly less offensive to Lady Fossle than his pink Aids ribbon.

The Mother at Rock

ALTHEA IS DEMENTED. Last night Tarquin, aged 15, was writhing in the sand dunes until 2am despite her impassioned text messages: 'Where R U?' and 'Cum hme NOW'. Fortunately, her texting skills, sparingly taught by Robbie, aged eight, aren't capable of translating 'Your father will thrash you if you do not get back to Seagull Cottage right this minute, you little toad.' She has already wrenched Jessica, aged 12, out of the Mariners' Arms, following a scary article in the *Daily Mail* about the cataclysmic effects of alcopops. Jessica said languidly, 'Mummy, you're just a saddo,' and blotted out the response with earphones and a Discman.

Althea indeed feels sad. She is dressed entirely from the Boden catalogue, with vast shirts covering up her fat bits, and pedal pushers to disguise the spider veins exploding on the inside of her knees. She wanted to do the cliff walk – 'Won't that be fun? It's so beautiful' – but Tarquin told her to get a life, and when she suggested a jolly picnic on Daymer beach, Jessica said that it was where the Holcrofts' dachshund drowned.

Suddenly, encased in her mail-order flowery frock, her waist gripped by a belt approximating chintz baler twine, she feels entirely superfluous to their lives. Tarquin wants blackcurrant vodka, Jessica wants black nail varnish and Robbie wants to go to his friend Josh who has a really cool mummy with a Porsche. Althea's hair is frizzy with the sea air and her Boots No 7 lipstick has drained into little tension lines around her mouth. All she wants in life is to stop anybody getting pregnant. And is Tarquin taking drugs? Althea knows it is a slippery slide from one Marlboro Light to injecting heroin. Connection and love is what the housemaster said, so at night she slinks past the Mariners', head down, clutching the mobile, trying not to be an embarrassing parent.

All she wants in life is to stop anybody getting pregnant

*Sybil has never felt the same about private views since she mistook
an art installation for a fire extinguisher*

The Gossips

DAPHNE AND SYBIL don't know what the Melange Gallery is coming to; the pictures are quite hideous. Sybil has never felt the same about private views since she mistook an art installation for a fire extinguisher; Daphne has resorted to smoking viciously at the landscapes. At home in Wiltshire, a landscape is a landscape, jolly nice frame and perfectly good pheasants winging across the canvas, not some nuclear disaster zone with pyres of dead sheep. And so they turn their backs on Fentiman Birtwhistle's exciting new acrylics to observe the humming throng. 'Celia Butter's daughter has just been put in the Priory, I hear. Apparently one has to share one's feelings with frightful people like soap opera stars. I must say, I'd be awfully cross if I was Celia – she gave the girl everything, and a nice education at Heathfield – but she's being marvellous.' Sybil's long nose twitches with the disapproval of one blessed with achingly dull children. Daphne is convinced that Charles Corbett's granddaughter has had an illegitimate child in Thailand – 'And there he is, dear Charles, talking to Lily Sweeting as if he doesn't have a care in the world.' Daphne's granddaughter wants to be a physiotherapist, something that appals her as it requires flat shoes and contact with the NHS. Sybil spots that Lord Corbett has bought a picture – the red dot is hovering above Birtwhistle's *Train Crash*. 'Pure kindness,' says Daphne, scooping up a passing canapé. 'One wouldn't even hang it in the lavatory.' The champagne is getting warm, and Sybil irritable. Charles Corbett hasn't so much as glanced in her direction; the Fitzwalters actually dodged behind a sculpture, and the absence of the Mortimers is remarkable. This is supposed to be an evening in aid of charity. 'Extraordinary,' says Sybil, 'the people who won't put their hands in their pockets.' At which point she and Daphne leave without buying a picture or tipping the cloakroom attendant for their ancient minks.

Abigail spreads herself over the whole sofa, sometimes filing the calluses on her feet

The Terrible Flatmate

ABIGAIL NEVER GOES out. At first, Katie and Charlotte thought this was completely brilliant because they don't ever have to put the burglar alarm on. Such a relief after the time Charlotte got trashed at Woody's and couldn't remember the number, so the alarm went off and the police came round to find her being sick in the umbrella stand. Abigail is hence regarded by Charlotte's mother as a reliable and steadying influence. Katie thinks it's great that Abigail buys the lavatory paper but does she have to be so weird? The month during which she was on the cabbage soup diet meant vats of boiling green ooze, and she writes her name on the yogurts in the fridge. Abigail, who teaches sociology, says that the demarcation of privacy is essential to mutual respect – and what about the time Katie got so cross with Charlotte's boyfriend for drinking her vodka? Abigail doesn't drink, so is utterly unsympathetic to Charlotte's epic hangovers: 'You only have yourself to blame, Charlotte, and might I suggest that you buy your own coffee in future?' Charlotte retaliates by tipping Abigail's greying bras – propped neatly across the bath on a foldaway clothes rack – into her dirty water. The atmosphere has been rather tense in Lavender Gardens ever since, particularly on the one night Katie and Charlotte were in and wanted to watch *EastEnders*, but Abigail had appropriated the television in order to watch a documentary on Third World debt. She always spreads herself over the whole sofa, sometimes filing the calluses on her feet with a pumice stone at the same time as answering the questions on *University Challenge*. Katie now calls her the Troll. When Abigail takes a shine to Charlotte's estate-agent boyfriend, and offers to soak lentils for them all and cook a free-range chicken ('I'll do the shopping and divide it three ways afterwards'), Charlotte mouths '*Single White Female*' behind her back.

The Minor
Stately Home Owners

GEORGE AND WIGGY inherited Gargoyles 15 years ago from George's spinster aunt Primrose. George had just been invalided from the Army, and was doing some damn fool job on Civvy Street, and Wiggy, being a good sort, didn't really mind the tap-tap-tap of the death-watch beetle or Lady Maud's ghost in the King's Bedchamber. Life at Gargoyles is lived on the front line versus the heritage police, the worm that has got into the Grinling Gibbons carvings (mentioned in Pevsner), and the bloody visitors.

George has to open the house, of course, to get the grants, but he conducts a cunning war of attrition with 40w bulbs and fossilised cobwebs. Guests actually staying at Gargoyles find arachnidan eco-systems under the beds in which Charles II et al once slept. Bleary with George's homemade cider (sold by Wiggy in the moathouse as Gargoyles' Gumption), they attempt to disengage the round-pin plug of the electric blanket which, combined with the damp, constitutes certain death. In the bathroom down a windswept corridor, past the small Van Dyck, hot water emerges fitfully in a peaty trickle. High above is a single-bar electric heater operated with a frayed string. Wiggy discourages anyone from staying in winter. She's used to dressing by the solid fuel range in the kitchen, but the ballcocks seize up in the loos and, only last February, their daughter's goldfish froze to death in its bowl. The fire in the Grand Salon has to have a two-foot layer of old ash before it will draw at all. He sees no need for central heating at Gargoyles. 'I've dedicated my life to getting rid of it,' he says merrily. 'Whenever I feel really depressed I get a spanner and rip out another radiator.'

Guests staying at Gargoyles find arachnidan eco-systems under the bed in which Charles II once slept

*One day she rang to say she would not be coming in because she
didn't have enough money for the Tube fare*

The Summer Intern

CRESSIDA IS DOING work experience at *Gloss* magazine because Daddy knows the editor. Yet she is magnificently unimpressed by her good fortune, and any attempt at work – a little light photocopying or fetching the art director's sandwiches – is severely impeded by the calls on her mobile. The trilling imperative of Cressida's social life permeates the entire office, making all privy to her plans to meet Hugo and Max at Crazy Larry's on Thursday. To ask Cressida to research a piece on designer flip-flops, Miss Gimlet had to stand by Cressida's desk for quite five minutes while she took a call from her boyfriend in Ibiza. 'Research' is a loose term to Cressida: she gets soooo bored with talking to PRs that she spends most of the time ringing Prizelines (about the only thing she uses the office telephone for, as calls cost £1.50 a minute). Her time-keeping is delightfully vague; indeed, one day she rang Miss Gimlet to say she would not be coming in because she didn't have enough money for the Tube fare. Since Cressida is the only person at *Gloss*, including the fashion editor, to have a genuine Hermès bag, this was considered a novel excuse. Maybe she has a future in creative writing. Everyone watches with stunned fascination as she takes three-hour lunches with her mother in Chelsea, then, after graciously returning for 20 minutes, has to leave early to get ready for a night with Fergus, James and Bels at Attica.

Youth after gilded youth drops in to see Cress, and flip through her copies of *Tatler* and *Elle* while they drink skinny lattes and plan their holiday in Corfu. They all trail out for sushi once Cressida has jammed the photocopier with the notes of the editorial meeting. Just as Miss Gimlet is about to Say Something, pictures are published of Cress sitting next to Prince William at a polo match. Then everyone agrees that life will really be quite dull after she leaves.

The Fathers' Race

BARNEY SILVERMAN has been in training for the great day since April. There is no such thing as coming second: losing is for wimps. It would never do to let Barney Junior down. George Weebil is appalled by this manifestation of American enthusiasm. Bloody New York bankers, who do they think they are, coming over here and inflating the property market by paying whacking prices in Kensington, so everyone else has to make do with Wandsworth, and then, to add insult to injury, annexing sports day at Thomas's? The last time George ran was for the 22 bus on his way to the Chelsea Flower Show. And he now feels dyspeptic after some very fine potted shrimps at the Turf. The bread and butter pudding was probably a mistake too, judging by the stretching and limbering Barney is conducting in his new sportswear. After the capital offence of appearing keen, George most disapproves of anything new and those trainer thingies in particular. The children are always wanting them – it drives Rowena potty – but they really cannot be considered footwear for grown-ups. This gumboil of a Yank probably has go-faster logos on his underpants.

Barney is now psyching himself up by standing on one foot and flexing the other against his thigh. The yummy mummies look traitorously interested; they are all still talking about Barney Junior's birthday party in a marquee set-dressed as Hogwarts School, with caged owls, live toads and tensile wires elevating little Barney.

The race begins. Shelley Silverman is poised with her new digital video camera to record the happy event. It is really most unfortunate that George's leather-soled brogue slips on the wet grass and accidentally trips Barney as he is about to breast the tape. The Weebil children will never be asked to the Silvermans' birthday parties again.

The last time George ran was for the 22 bus on his way to the Chelsea Flower Show

Phoebe finds candlelight is much kinder on the dust

The Sloths

SELL-BY DATES hold no fears for Phoebe and Octavian. Phoebe knows perfectly well when the milk is off because the cats refuse to drink it. Octavian finds plucking pheasants much easier when they're really high – the feathers just fall out. Neither is remotely concerned about the tidal-wave of ironing; darling Mrs Hathaway will take a run at it on Wednesday. By which time it will be pointless Phoebe unpacking her weekend case, because the weekend will very nearly be there again. Besides, Snowdrop, who has a phantom pregnancy, is using it as a basket. Visitors to the house in Highgate approach with caution, picking their way over a panoply of mail-order roses – Phoebe had a marvellous time with the Hilliers catalogue but neglected to realise the follow-through required by October planting. Absolute death to her Emma Hope shoes.

Once past the roses, and the bulbs (also gasping to be planted), and the empties waiting to be recycled, guests are enveloped in a warm fug of claret, cat and candles. Phoebe finds candlelight is much kinder on the dust. Octavian has no truck with gas switch-on-the-logs-in-the-grate; there is a telltale line of debris across the carpet (and on his velvet dressing-gown, which doubles as a smoking jacket) where he has hauled lengths of damp oak to the fireplace. Fortunately Octavian's claret is awfully good, and eyes smarting with smoke rarely notice the pawmarks in the butter. Phoebe is a lavish cook – there are several cartons of cream, plus custodian cats, on the sideboard – and her pheasant is marinated in Calvados and apple for days, as she forgets about it. The mashed potato has 10 cloves of garlic – she was crushing while absorbed on the telephone – and is gold with olive oil Octavian buys from Soho on his way to the Garrick. After dinner they look thoughtfully at the washing up, Octavian has another cigar and Phoebe reads a novel.

The Schoolgirl Model

Posy was spotted in Claire's Accessories on the King's Road by Martine from Tempest, who instantly recognised her potential as a baby giraffe. Posy's nose is also small and pert. Tempest decrees that it's a nose that can wreck the face. 'A blobby end is death, dear,' said Martine. Posy agrees that blobby is gross. The height thing is wicked, as her brothers call her Treetop (how sad is that?), and the only advantage so far was that their spotty, dwarfy schoolfriends couldn't reach up to snog her at the Feathers Ball. Martine and Posy's mother are locked in battle about Posy's braces. Tessa Purefoy says that over her dead body are they coming off early, after all the money she's paid the dentist. Posy will just have to keep her mouth shut in photographs. And Posy isn't to sign anything without showing her first. Posy says, 'Cool, Mum', and drifts up to her bedroom, lighting joss sticks to cover the smell of cigs while she does her homework. A Marlboro Light is the slippery slope to the Priory as far as Mrs Purefoy is concerned. 'If I hear anything about anorexia or cocaine, Martine, that is absolutely it. *Finito*. I wasn't born yesterday. What is this magazine *Dazed and Confused* anyway?'

When Posy brought the Polaroid home it looked suspiciously as if she'd been photographed in an outfit made of eagle feathers, with one breast exposed. It seems only yesterday that Posy was wearing smocked dresses, now she's cutting the waistbands off £80 jeans with nail scissors to show the tattoo below her hipline. During London Fashion Week she makes only guest appearances at school. 'It's OK, Mum, I'm taking my revision to castings.' Indeed, her file on classical civilisation dwells in the deep litter of a knapsack among Ice White chewing-gum wrappers, mobile, Stila lip gloss, crisps, a spare thong and her lucky rabbit. The allure of GCSEs is dim compared with becoming the new face of Topshop.

*Posy looked suspiciously as if she'd been photographed in an outfit
made of eagle feathers, with one breast exposed*

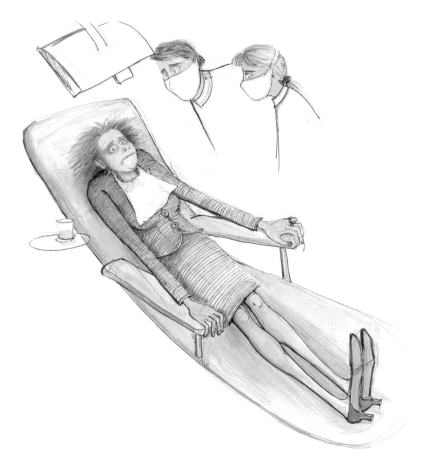

A phenomenal amount of rubble is wrapping itself round her tongue which, as the result of the injection, now feels the size of a cabbage

The Dental Patient

Is IT GOING to be the rack, the thumbscrew or the drill? Rosemary Winslow has recurrent memories of acute dental torture as a small child. She chipped a tooth as a teenager, having a nasty fall carrying her mother's shopping, and for years endured a yellowing corner on her front molar rather than brave a crown. Many have told her that dentistry is not as it was, that it is now caring and painless, but even as Mr Hatherop advances upon her in his mask, flexing latex gloves and carrying a syringe, she is overcome. 'Come, come, Mrs Winslow, there will only be a little prick,' he says in muffle-speak from behind the mask, jabbing a painkiller into her jaw – agony – at precisely the wrong moment. 'Well, well, Mrs Winslow, you certainly have a powerful bite there. Now, are we wearing our mouth guard? I see from your notes that you are a grinder at night.' Rosemary has long ago thrown away her mouth guard, since she would rather shoot herself in the mouth than wear something plastic that accumulates hideous yellow deposits in its moulded cavities. Nor can she respond to Mr Hatherop's jocund inquiries while he is grouting around top left. A phenomenal amount of rubble is wrapping itself round her tongue which, as the result of the injection, now feels the size of a cabbage.

In Rosemary Winslow's fevered imagination, while she is trying to keep her mouth open, exchange small talk with Mr Hatherop and concentrate on not being terribly sick, her tongue is now so big that it has slithered down the stairs, out of the door and gone shopping in Waitrose. And all the while Mr Hatherop is saying, 'Could we open a little wider, Mrs Winslow?' and talking of teeth whitening. 'Not that you don't have very nice teeth, considering your age.' It is at this point that she wrenches the paper bib from her dribbling chin, stuffs her tongue back in her mouth, drools and runs to lunch, where she can only drink soup through a straw.

Buffy makes a daily pitstop at Witchett's, marvellous camaraderie, haven of peace and quiet, smoked salmon and nursery food

The Gentlemen's Club Member

BUFFY PILKINGTON HAS been a member of Witchett's since he came out of the Guards. His godfather put him up, said he'd need to have a retreat from the womenfolk. 'Marvellous people, women, and your Julia is a charmer, but take my advice, old boy: avoid the baby stuff. It's very dodgy to be at home around 6pm, squalling and sticky fingers are much better left to old Nanny. Have a swift one in Witchett's, read the *Evening Standard*, chew the fat with the chaps and by the time you get home you can kiss downy heads and Julia will have had a bath.' Ever since, Buffy has made a daily pitstop at Witchett's, marvellous camaraderie, haven of peace and quiet, smoked salmon and nursery food – what more does a fellow want? He often goes to dinner now – Julia being down in the country with her horses – and queues patiently at the top of the stairs for Gracie to tick his name off. 'Evening, m'lord.' One evening, when he was with Miles Kilbride, he joshed her, saying, 'Now, Gracie, you don't know which lord I am, do you?' 'No m'lord, but you are on table three.'

Simple and uncomplicated, that's Witchett's. Plus a dash of louche romanticism. On the day of the Countryside March Buffy was standing, tweeded to the gills, in the morning room where Beau Brummell made such play with his lorgnette, when Miles battled in from Green Park saying, 'My God, I've seen a lot of shits.' And Buffy replied, quick as a flash, 'Were they in here or out there?' Sort of thing you can say without fear, Witchett's still having a sense of humour untrammelled by political correctitude. The last bastion where the harrumph of members reading *The Daily Telegraph* transcends the cheep of the mobile. A bolthole with damn fine cigars and immaculate discretion – an oasis. Only the other day Buffy heard the porter saying firmly on the hall telephone, 'No madam, no member's wife's husband is ever in the club.'

The Caravanners

A NICE QUEUE has built up behind Len and Sheila's caravan on the narrow, tricky bit of the A303 just beyond Stonehenge. Len is entirely oblivious to the boiling wake of road rage they're creating, since he and Sheila have been congratulating themselves on the success of Len's new stabiliser in limiting bounce. Mind you, it does help if you drive in the middle of the road.

At the next Little Chef, Len is going to stop and check the tow-hitch. Besides, Sheila needs the lav. Then they can all have some restorative egg and chips before the last leg of the journey to Dorset, and those challenging narrow lanes. This year they're going to ever such a pretty caravan park above Chesil Beach. According to *Mobile Home Monthly*, it's in a position of unrivalled natural beauty, with power-point connections and mains water. The children asked why they couldn't go to Majorca like everyone else at school but Len said England was good enough for him, thank you, so it was good enough for them, and he didn't want any lip, see? Dorset is a fine place, and they'll be going to the Swannery at Abbotsbury to see the Queen's swans. Now you couldn't do that in some fancy foreign place, could you? They've got the DVD player and young Steve has brought his Sony PlayStation, which makes Julie cry because he won't let her play with it, so it's just like home. Sheila says she surely hopes the rain keeps off, because she doesn't want to spend all her holiday at the launderette in Bridport.

Arriving, having caused a leisurely bottleneck for the final 10 miles, Len is delighted to see the folks next door only have a TV aerial – not, like them, a dish. And their striped awning is vastly inferior to Sheila's sunburst pattern. Only when it comes to jacking up the 'cara' does Len discover that he's left the jack handle at home in Pinner.

It helps if you drive in the middle of the road

The rest of her life stretches before her as a monochrome corridor of emotional nullity

The Jilted Girlfriend

THERE IS A nanosecond as Joanne wakes each morning when she thinks all is right with the world and that the stars are God's daisy chain, but then she remembers. Her stomach knots, her chest heaves under the dead cat of depression, and her bare feet sink into the clammy pile of damp Kleenex beside the bed. Giles has dumped her. She can never be happy again. The rest of her life stretches before her as a monochrome corridor of emotional nullity – an existential version of an Ian Schrager hotel – from here on to the grave. As she was telling Daisy on the phone last night, and then Alice when Daisy had to go out, and then Rose when Alice had to watch *Friends*, her future is meaningless without Giles. She wanted to have his babies. They could have had a little cottage in the country and she'd have cooked Sunday lunch while he played golf. Rose pointed out that the nearest Joanne has ever got to cooking is the Pizza Express delivery number, so what's with the domestic goddess thing all of a sudden? And golf . . . So that was why Giles wore those awful sweaters. 'No, Jo, don't cry. But do you really want to marry someone whose favourite song is *Drop Kick Me, Jesus, Through the Goal Posts of Life?*'

Jo, distraught from smoking and vodka, is inconsolable. Why, oh why, did he leave? If only he would ring, she'll never leave her tights to dry over the bath again. Or be late for Arnold Schwarzenegger movies. And she'll always help his mother with the washing-up. It was probably his mother's fault, awful old bag. Alice said that Giles was spotted groping a girl at Pitcher & Piano. Oh God. Has anyone seen the bastard? Daisy and Alice say she is absolutely not to ring him. So of course she does, and the new answering machine message says, 'Giles and Daisy are not at home right now . . .' Jo gets a new haircut, loses a stone, hits DKNY and everyone says she looks fabulous and Giles was just a boring accountant anyway.

'We're only going to stay in Norfolk, for heaven's sake, not Siberia.'

The Man Packing the Boot

COLIN IS ADAMANT. Pained, but implacable: this is man's work. 'Stop. Stop, everyone. Leave this to me. It has to be done scientifically. No, Lottie, do not put your guinea-pig in the glove pocket.' He then takes out everything that his wife has bunged in – and which fitted admirably, given a good shove – rearranging the entire contents on the pavement with the precision of an army exercise. Molly recognises the same didactic that consumes her husband when loading the dishwasher. ('Can I just show you? If you put the plates in this way round, you'll get much more in.') Colin has now hit his head on the tailgate and is roaring for Elastoplast. This necessitates taking out the cases he's just put back in, because the first aid kit is below the boot in the spare wheel compartment. 'Molly, I don't know why you have to take all this stuff. We're only going to stay with the Brocklebanks, and in Norfolk, for heaven's sake, not Siberia.' Molly says crisply that the heating at the Brocklebanks is such that it might as well be Siberia, and stuffs her electric blanket into his arms. 'I am not sleeping in a cold bed, Colin, even if Conky Brocklebank is your oldest friend. And don't forget the Wellingtons. Don't shout, it upsets Lottie.' Colin, tight-lipped, packs Barbours and bottles of wine for dear old Conky into every crevice. 'There, easily done,' he says, triumphantly forcing the door shut. 'You just have to know how.' The whole lot is disinterred on the Embankment because Lottie can't find her GameBoy, then they have to return to the house as Colin's smoking jacket has been left in the hall. 'If you'd just let me get on with it, Colin darling, I'd have known exactly where everything was.' It is on the M11 that the guinea-pig escapes down the heating duct, little legs thrashing. Lottie becomes hysterical and the RAC has to be called. It's midnight before they arrive at the Brocklebanks.

The Pony Club Official

Viv has an eagle eye for mothers cheating in the flag race. As the children fly round on their Thelwells there is always the one – usually Marie Pinchbeck – who'll surreptitiously pick up a dropped flag and hand it back to their darling thinking Viv isn't looking. It was a very happy day when Viv recommended little Tiffany Pinchbeck, as spoilt and rude a child as she's ever encountered, to a neighbouring Pony Club as 'a marvellously competitive rider'. The paint on the jumps may be peeling, but Viv is not going to have the Chalfont Foliat branch polluted by minxes. What's more, Mrs Pinchbeck did not even thank her for unblocking the Portapotty in Tiffany's horsebox at the last Pony Club camp, after Tiffany had smuggled Bacardi Breezers in for all her friends on the last night. Viv has an innate sense of fair play; eight-year-old Susie Spall is unlikely to become Mary King, but she's shown keen interest in Viv's Pony-for-the-Day classes in stable management and her father, who has a nice painting business, has been most generous in sponsoring the working hunter class. Then there's Lady Sybilla's daughter, dear Rachel, for whose birthday party Viv helped build a cross-country course and measured out the dressage ring with washing lines, gently suggesting that it would make the party go with more of a swing if Rachel didn't win everything.

Viv has known them all since they were tots, bless them, at her riding school, built out of breeze blocks by Alan, her husband, who's an insurance salesman during the week, primarily to remove himself from a household of women who smell of saddle soap. Next month Viv's been asked to be a jump steward at the BHS Pre-Novice event at Wolverton: it will be a splendid day with her Thermos, sandwiches, deckchair and clipboard.

Viv measured out the dressage ring with washing lines

He gives his best lectures on Irish Georgian houses fuelled by Jameson's

The Irish Aristocrat

THE PURPLE KNIGHT of Clon is delighted to welcome *Hello!* into his beautiful home. It will pay for the repairs to the library, the only room with a consistently roaring fire. Everywhere else at Clongargle is ossified with cold and damp, so as a result the Clons are fabulously well read, having spent their lives tucked up with a succession of smelly old Labradors on the collapsing library sofas. Saffron, the Knight's supermodel granddaughter, who is going out with the son of a Rolling Stone, is photographed with the Knight in the yellow drawing-room, the sunken garden, the morning-room and the long gallery. The latter posed considerable difficulties as there are so many gaps on the wall where the pictures have been sent to Christie's. The Knight has sold all but his gloomiest ancestors, and had high hopes of flogging the family Sèvres, but his housekeeper is so blind now she's chipped all the cups while dusting.

Still, Clongargle wouldn't be the same without Mrs McGinty. She and the Knight are entirely happy with the unbroken continuity of her filthy food, most of which he has shot or fished and all of which comes with boiled potatoes. The Knight considers any complaints to be an affectation, so the Clons are all very thin, and beat a hasty retreat from the dining-room back to the library and the whiskey tray. The Knight doesn't notice as his bloodstream, particularly after a day's racing at Gowran Park, is 20 per cent proof. He gives his best lectures on Irish Georgian houses fuelled by Jameson's. The Georgian furniture at Clongargle is fabled, and experts brave staying at the house to admire it. The man from the Metropolitan Museum was astonished, when getting a glass of water in the kitchen at night, to see Mrs McGinty emerging in her nightie from the boiler room. She has always slept there, she said, it being the only warm room in the house.

The Woman with the Filthy Car

ZARA IS WHIZZING through Piddle Bagpuize on her way home from the school run and a bikini wax when she sees Mr Pettifer outside the post office, which is also the delicatessen. She stops to offer him a lift because, bless him, he's collecting signatures to Save Our Shop. Zara *so* agrees because where else would she be able to get first-class stamps and buffalo mozzarella? It is, indeed, the remains of a Piddle Bagpuize Post Office organic tomato ciabatta sandwich that's stuck in the gearshift. 'Jump in!' she cries, sweeping Hagrid off the front seat. Mr Pettifer tentatively regards the deep litter of crumpled Kleenex, toys, kitten heels and Polo mints. There's a sporting chance of severe internal injury from sitting on a Carmen roller, hastily discarded by Zara the previous evening as she arrived at dinner with the Fotheringhams. An ominous crunch as he lowers himself into the front seat signifies that he's crushed a half-eaten packet of rice cakes. Hagrid, horrified to be ejected from the front seat, now pants dog breath over Mr Pettifer's shoulder.

Mozart is trilling from Zara's radio – 'I do love Classic FM, don't you Mr Pettifer?' – as she swings down Gypsy Lane, causing a seismic shift of improving novels, pearls and Marlboro Lights on the dashboard. Mr Pettifer gamely fields a pair of Versace sunglasses. Feet braced against the floor (a combination of terror and the adhesive properties of old chewing-gum), he survives the journey to Rose Cottage and disentangles himself from Zara's car clutching a doll and one Nike trainer. Zara is mortified to see that his dignified, charcoal worsted-clad back is now covered in ginger Hagrid hair. She must get the car cleaned. At the first intimation of spring, a flurry of potato crisps will be expelled from the air conditioning.

She swings down Gypsy Lane, causing a seismic shift of improving novels, pearls and Marlboro Lights on the dashboard

'Don't forget your ski passes, sun screen, goggles, gloves and hat'

The Family Skiing Holiday

KIRSTY IS SOOOO embarrassed. Mummy has insisted she goes to ski school with awful Jean-Claude and his boring 'Bend ze knees'. It's so rank. Caspar's allowed to go snowboarding – it's just not fair. Dad roused them all at 7.30am. 'Wakey, wakey! Don't forget your ski passes, sun screen, goggles, gloves and hat.' And then Mum came in, all bright and thinking she looks like Claudia Schiffer in a mobile duvet, saying, 'Hello darlings, it's a glorious day, we're meeting the Weymouths for lunch at Le Blanchot. Now, don't forget your ski passes, sun screen, goggles, gloves and hat.' Little Bertie got up all bouncy and sweet – so he got crispy bacon, but Caspar and Kirsty were so late they landed the rubbery scrambled egg, and Kirsty is terrified that Sophie Weymouth, who's in her class at St Mary's, Calne, will see her being packed off to Jean-Claude by Dad in his minging deerstalker and spotty hankie-scarf. Why can't he be like Sophie's father in black Gore-Tex? Just as Kirsty was checking her ski pass, sun screen, goggles, gloves and hat, she discovered a major zit. Where's her Eve Lom Dynamite? This is a crisis. It'll have to be Fed-Exed. And Dad says, 'Come on, Kirsty, Jean-Claude's never going to notice that you've got terminal acne' – which is just pathetic – 'Have you got your ski pass, sun screen, goggles, gloves and hat?' God, parents are soooo one-track. Mummy is in a panic about how to stop Kirsty underage drinking in Dick's T-Bar ('Oh, Mum, get a life – you don't give me enough money for a start') and whether Caspar will fall down a crevasse while snowboarding, headphones blasting. Only Bertie is her little snow bunny, winning his bronze medal in Snow Kids. Afterwards, everyone says they had a lovely time, thank you. 'Well, we hope you did, because it was jolly expensive.' And when Mum goes to Sainsbury's the children all shout, 'Have you got your reward card, bag, car keys, gloves and hat?'

The Yoga Fanatic

THERE WAS A TIME when Naomi didn't know the Flying Crow pose from Russell Crowe, but now she has embraced the path of physical well-being, emotional balance and spiritual growth, or rather 'being presented to the flow of one moment to the next', as her yoga teacher calls it. Naomi 'oms' in the office, which is very tiresome for everyone else trying to use the coffee machine. 'I am part of life's joyful sound,' she says beatifically, holding her fingers and thumbs in little circles. Anita from accounts is most put out. 'You may be filling yourself with luminous energy, but what about my cappuccino?' Naomi tells her to let it go.

On holiday, all lithe and eager, she uses the beach as a yoga studio, maddening for those who hoped the Cobra and the Downward Dog were cocktails with little parasols. Naomi drinks only flat mineral water to keep her inner self pure, and speaks in mantras, which caused a certain amount of confusion when she told the gorgeous Aussie barman, 'I am balanced and secure, open to new possibilities', and he mistook it for a chat-up line. While everyone else is slobbing out with rubbish novels, Naomi is reading *The Path to Holistic Health* and has doubled herself into the Hare pose to anoint the soles of her feet with factor 25. Back at the office, she meditates while reading her e-mail, 'The Zen master says make haste slowly, Anita', and stands on one leg in the lift to focus her inner strength before meetings. When she first started meditating all she could think about was shopping lists, and how her flat needed decorating, and Brian in marketing's bad breath. Now she's painted the flat white, sits cross-legged on a cushion and says, 'I give myself permission to go within and re-energize.' The yoga teacher says that when shopping list thoughts arise Naomi is to acknowledge them, then return to her breathing, and empty her mind of all but lotus blossoms.

'I give myself permission to go within and re-energize'

The Embarrassing Parents*

DICK AND PATSY can mouth all the words to *American Pie*. Groovers in the Sixties (actually, it was the Seventies, but Patsy says that counts as the Sixties up until the Sex Pistols), they still deploy the gyratory tactics refined at their white-tie university disco. Patsy's knees crack like pistol shots when she affects the twist – not that anyone can hear above *La Bamba* – and her arm movements are those of a demented chicken. Dick pokes the air with fingernails gnarled from bedding out, and shakes his head so vigorously that dandruff is expelled by centrifugal force.

At multi-generational parties, their daughters just pray Dad won't hit the champagne sufficiently to do his Elvis impersonation. It's bad enough when the parents sing along to *YMCA*, together with wiggly hip movements – don't they know it's a gay anthem? Then there's the grim certainty that Dick and Patsy will clear the floor during Gloria Gaynor's *I Will Survive*; at Aunt Molly's 40th birthday party they cannon off the dance floor, break a perfectly good table lamp, and the family doctor is moved to ask Granny if there's any history of epilepsy in the family. Come midnight – and *Jumping Jack Flash* – Dick, who is now sweating profusely, twangs an imaginary guitar and makes little leaps in the air. Thus Aunt Molly sustains a nasty cut on her shin from the flying heel of his Mr Bally evening shoe. Patsy, shoulders jiggling like piston engines, inadvertently embraces a cheese plant hired from Palmy Nights, and Dick shrugs his dinner jacket off to halfway down his back and struts like a bandaged baboon in order to give *The Winner Takes it All* some welly. On the way home in the car, the kids say, 'Mum, Dad, you are soooo embarrassing. Why can't you just grow up?'

*Illustration on front of jacket